Herbert W. Rode

DEPRESSION

My way into the deep… and again out!

Herbert W. Rode

DEPRESSION

My way into the deep…
…and again out!

Prologue

First:
Please notice that the original version of this book is in German language: "Mein Weg ins Tief - und wieder raus!. - Depressionen") - . It was not professionally translated and being so, it is possible that some mistakes appear in it.

Betrayed in marriage - divorce - "war of roses" - loss of workplace - suicide of new significant other - loss of property --- excessive perspiration, panic attacks, dissociative disorders, depression, high blood pressure, migraine attack --- therapies --- new goals, fresh start···

What lies in front of you is not a medically reasoned disquisition. It is more than a brief description of a part of one chapter in my life - about 25 years - in which my life's journey led me into an unforeseen low, but also how I found my way out of it again.

Today I am mid-60. I kept in touch with depression over the years, which has changed my life very much. On my way there, I did not notice any of the signs of this terrible disorder. In the lowest phase I lost almost everything what my life was and what was supporting it.

And of course I slowly came back on a path that significantly helped me. So, I am able to say today, that I could break away from this disorder: "DEPRESSION".

My life changed again, into the present, in a positive way.

I do not describe my "story" fully detailed. I tried to write only about the essential events and circumstances that led me into the abyss and back out of it. Maybe one or another recognizes oneself. Everyone who blunders into a low has their own path and their own "story" for it, but many of the symptoms that accompany you down that path are similar, if not the same. Maybe I can help one or another to distinguish the signs. A good piece of advice from me is, if you feel that there is something inside of you that drags you in a negative direction, go and consult with a doctor and try to talk about it in all honesty and confidentiality···

In this, what lies in front of you, I have anonymized all persons – including myself as well as professions, places, etc. This is important to me. It is about the consequences of wrongdoings in my life and the consequences that resulted from them. It is about my encounter with a deceitful disorder: DEPRESSION!

A nice proverb by Sören Kierkegaard

'Life can only be understood backwards; but it must be lived forwards.'

Signs

I need to get out of here··· I need to get away··· I cannot stay here···this happiness is crushing me··· please come with me!'

– Those were vaguely the words to Dorit (all names are changed), my ex, about 15 years ago. We were at the wedding reception of our friends' daughter at that moment, in a barn of a farm that was specially prepared for celebrations like this. It was almost midnight and Dorit insistently told me that there would be a surprise at midnight and the wedding cake etc. etc. etc··· Everything left me extremely cold. I did not recognize myself like that! – Earlier we were dancing and had a lot of fun, until Dorit danced a little too intensively with one of her colleagues. In the past it had never bothered me much and on that night I couldn't really explain it to myself but that happiness seemed like a tight corset – almost suffocating me, squeezing my soul – all positive emotions were as if they were frozen.

After all I could convince Dorit to go home with me. The next day everything was okay again. Whatever had happened to me the night before seemed as blown away and I felt embarrassed about the way I had reacted. – Back then I had no idea that this had something to do with depression. Depression, I knew the word, but not much else about it!

How did I get to this point and later even further and deeper?

It was the year 1999 and we were already married for 25 years. We had two nearly grown up children. Both of us were in good positions at our jobs and we had built up a good life for us over the years – with a beautiful house and vacations wherever we wished. Both our kids had almost completed their high school and their career goals seemed promising for both of them.

9

If you constantly scratch a thick rope with a sharp knife even that thick rope will eventually become thinner and finally rip⋯ - that was what happened to my soul!

Dorit always had ambitions to flirt with other men and she enjoyed the attributes of those men who showed interest. At the beginning of our marriage – middle of the 70' s – she started cheating on me. A huge coincidence had made me aware of that serious slip. After a night shift at my employers' I wanted to go to my car in the morning to drive home. Just in that moment I saw the car of a friend passing by the firm – in the car was Dorit, too, whose way to work also passed by here. Both of them did not notice that I had seen them. But only in the evening I could confront Dorit, who confessed then all of it. They had spent the night together in our apartment⋯ The friendship with her nightly bedfellow broke off, but I held on to my marriage with Dorit, because I loved her very much, I did not want to give up because of that. We were married for just about a year then⋯

In the following 15 years our children were born. I made immense progress in my career and we built a house. After selling the first house, we set our goals even higher and built a more beautiful and bigger house in a better location.

The tornado of our life and our love carried us away. We had our goals and our paths found them.

However this all did not go without obstacles and burdens.

Back then there was still a period of high interest rates – 12 % - and the rate loan payments for our house were high. When our first child was on the way back in the end of the 70' s and Dorit stopped working I started searching for a new job while I was still working in my secure job which I loved, so I could earn more money. – I started fieldwork and was later promoted to sales manager. I earned more, had a company car and other benefits – but in hindsight I have to say that this job did not fulfill me – I resigned to my fate to be there for my family, even in this matter. Only after about 15 years – in the mid 90's – our financial situation developed positively, also because I had been changing employers repeatedly and did better financially and because my ex was also back to work.

If you had to carry the burden of this kind of financial situation for 15 years you can either be broken or strengthened. I think I was strengthened in that matter since we had dug our way into the light, with many shovels and a lot of energy. Our future was financially promising and at that time our family life was generally nice from any point of view.

How it all started

The 80´s. Dorit and I led a nice open life also in premises of our sexual life. Open means: we could talk about everything and act out our wishes and phantasies together. Sex with others was off the table . However Dorit hadn' t changed and still enjoyed her own charm that was so appealing to other men. She flirted and coquetted – on the Internet I found to 'coquet' the following:

'needing to get the attention from others, also to arouse erotic interest and to make oneself interesting' – and that applied to 100% to Dorit. She was like that, also professionally. She wanted to be the first in line, to be the best – which isn' t wrong, except if you wonder, in which of way?

What kind of impact those attributes had on me at the time. I knew Dorit for nearly 20 years now and up to a certain point I could live with it. It was always important to me that I would have never felt hurt by the way Dorit acted. Mainly it was like that but even back then in the 70' s and 80' s, there were moments that touched my soul and not positively – but I just suppressed those feelings, got over them···

··· and then: At the end of the 80' s, Dorit was part of the parents council of our daughters school – of course she told me about the activities that occurred there and that she was supposed to organize the graduation party together with another father (Axel) of that class. No problem. They met every now and then to discuss necessary topics. Also no problem – not yet – well, until Dorit entrusted me that there was sexual tension between them. Dorit then started arguing that she was so young when we both met for the first time – she was 15 then – and that she was missing something, sexually. For me it wasn' t different, for me Dorit was also the only one I had ever had sex with and at least she had had a slip right at the beginning of our marriage.

We talked a lot about this topic and at some point I gave in –
what an idiot (today I know that). How can I explain that about
myself? I always wanted to give Dorit everything, so that she
would be satisfied with our life – it was too much! We agreed on
the term that it could only be this one time⋯ even when
discussed everything about Axel beforehand, he should know that
I knew about everything and that I allowed it only once. A
freedom in a marriage which is hard to explain, only that I let this
happen out of love – that was how I perceived it!

Eventually it happened between them and after that, the topic was
over for a long time. I told Dorit that I did not wish to be
'cheated' , that it would be the biggest violation and if she
would ever have those wishes again, I needed to know because
that was the only way we could handle the whole situation⋯
however.

Signs of depression

In what state was I when Dorit got intimate with Axel? I was aware of it and in those hours, when Dorit was gone, it was the first time I had to deal with anxiety. Later I could analyze it better – later, when I knew more about this, when I had more knowledge about depression. This condition, anxiety, touched my soul negatively and hurt it, too. – Eventually, this wasn't going to be the last time.

Casually, you go and discover something that brings up big questions. – When I came home some weeks after that 'happening' I found a strange key behind one of the cushions on the sofa, just by coincidence. I asked Dorit about it and only by her reaction I could tell that something was wrong. That fact immediately stung me in my stomach and my soul. Dorit reported that Axel had come to visit and that it had happened again and she asked for my forgiveness and assured me that it would never happen again etc. etc. etc··· - and I forgave her. As she knew how she could compensate me, it happened very intensely on the couch, or was it on the carpet--- our children slept already and everything was 'done' pretty fast···

··· Dorit and Axel were also done then – as far as I know.

The next year – 1991 – passed by without problems in that matter. We allowed ourselves our first vacation by plane and got to know a nice family from the former DDR with whom we kept in touch after for many years. – For me this contact still exists, after 25 years.

As I have written before, Dorit and I discussed our everyday topics and not everyday topics very well. At least that was how I saw it! 'Freedom' is also linked to openness and honesty. This 'freedom' that I still felt, her coquetting, was simply part of her. On the other hand, honesty from both sides was even more crucial now that she had 'cheated' again and it turned to be a major element in our lives. One sees an agreement this way and another that way··· I assume that Dorit saw our agreement on honesty a little bit different. Maybe for her it was like a 'pressure', she never told me···?

An Avalanche started rolling

Definitely, many things took their courses for us. We enjoyed more financial freedom, we had financial goals and fulfilled ourselves one or another wish we had for a long time and our very discreet married life things went in the right direction. Maybe it had to do with my knowledge that other men desired my wife as well, I was nearly always hot for her and we lived out one or more of our lusts quite intensively. - Was it maybe all scheming of my ex? She told me more and more about two of her colleagues. The same level and procedure as before: Openness about flirts··· ' I don't want it to become more', I told her 'but if something happens, I don't want to be cheated on - I want you to be honest with me and tell me about things so we can manage somehow together!' - From today's viewpoint, this was a major mistake, I always left a door open for Dorit and it happened again. 3-4-5-6-7 times every year in the entire 90's.

There were other men, even some of our close acquaintances. I got more and more insecure and I lost continuously my self-confidence. My soul was vibrating over every thought I had over Dorit and her sexual experiences. It still came to our talks to bring everything out in the open - not every little detail, but too much. She raved about the enormous manhood of one or two and I wanted to compete. I also wanted to have more to offer to her sexually and to satisfy her, so that she would not have these wishes of extramarital sex anymore··· I did not manage to do so. Many things in our marriage became more critical now, especially as I became more insecure. I lost trust and started controlling everything much more··· Back then we had no mobile phones yet. I could monitor landline phone calls with a program on my computer. I prepared items in our living area so that I would notice if something had changed··· etc. etc. etc. I wanted to know, if she was cheating on me and obviously Dorit felt very controlled.

In those times it occurred more and more that I started to perspire excessively. In countless situations: standing in line at the supermarket, at the hairdresser while waiting under the gown, at the dentist also while waiting under the gown and also every morning when I got ready for work and I put on my tie. I left the tie of more and more then – it was suitable in those times as we people started to wear business casual clothing. I also perspired excessively if I had to go down for breakfast after a night in a hotel. My shame and insecurity, due to the perspiration, the wet sweat on my forehead, everybody is looking at you – lead to me avoiding these situations as well. Years later I found out that this avoidance mechanism was the big mistake for those attacks. You get deeper and deeper into that low and the process of the symptoms becomes vigorous.

Along with the extreme perspiration came more and more back pains. Muscles always work when experiencing psychological problems so that it easily leads to cramps in the muscle areas. Here you usually first find other causes: too much sitting, wrong body posture, etc. ⋯ - The mind has big influence on the entire physical perception. That is something I know in hindsight and the body finds the weak spots⋯

Other venues of life – more unexpected problems – end of a marriage

For Dorit and me then however came a time of more peace and calm. We maintained our friendships. Visits here and visits there. Our children were of course also significantly important in our lives. Dorit had a very close relationship to both of them, but the most to our son.

One day an incident about our daughter hit us very hard. She tried to suicide with a cocktail of pills. It ended well but then she escaped from the hospital. An unimaginably difficult situation! It was end of July and we received the call from the hospital in the evening. I immediately left to search for her wherever I could think of – I did not find her. At midnight came another call from the hospital informing us that she had returned. That took loads of our minds. But the rough times of puberty of both children accompanied us on at all times – absolutely not easy with all that other stress going on.

I want to get back once more to the situations, to the insecurities, to the times of distrust. Whether I was out during the day, whether I was sleeping over elsewhere over night or whether I was on our yearly fall vacation with our son on a small island in Denmark and also whether my ex had some appointments in the evening – I was always followed by anxiety.

In the beginning I wrote: 'If you constantly scratch a thick rope with a sharp knife, even that thick rope will eventually become thinner and finally rip⋯'

From 1999 – 2001 I had quite unexplainable health problems. I was diagnosed with 'dissociative disorder' after I went to see a doctor after some of these 'attacks'. In the following I quote from WIKIPEDIA:

'The brain generates a track of our experiences out of many of our impressions like visual, auditory, tactile, olfactory, gustatory, proprioceptive and kinesthetic signals. To do so the signals that arrive in many different places in the brain have to be processed and integrated. The track of experiences that is generated through that process is sorted by space and time and saved into memory. Due to the high skills of processing and integration in the human brain this process is experienced within the individual as an entity. In reality on the other hand many factors are necessary to connect mental processes and contents to preserve these experiences. Are two or more of these mental processes or contents therefore these experiences not connected anymore although this is supposed to be the case we speak of dissociation. This can occur in everyday life as a normal dissociative phenomenon but also as a psychological disorder which then impairs the functionality of the individual.'

How did I experience the disorders? I fell into a kind of 'absence' to completely diverging times. I switched off. For about 30 minutes. Apparently I got really quiet in those times and some sort of daydreams started playing inside my mind. I could only remember that I had seen something like 'dragons' ⋯ nothing bad happened during those perceptions, except that those 'dragons' were buzzing through my head. Afterwards I could hardly put into words what I had experienced; I just couldn't find the words to describe it ‒ besides I had no energy, no power, for hours. Within 2 years I had these 'attacks' 10-12 times. I got a thorough examination in a clinic. Physically I was in top shape. Finally I told the doctor about my problems with Dorit. From the clinic I became as explanation that these problems caused enormous stress to my brain and that this 'dissociative disorder' could be explained as result of those issues- it was like a short circuit in electricity terms. For me, it became clear that I had to finish with my wife's 'ambitions'.

In 1999 we celebrated our silver wedding anniversary. Despite everything this celebration was okay for Dorit and me. Problems occurred and it was because of our son was more and more crazy. Here and there he became very hot-tempered. For example, on our silver wedding anniversary he had a dispute with his older sister. He raged so much that he threw a big iron ring towards her, which then landed on our car. Later we, or better I, had many more problems with our son. He even had to switch schools because he was verbally aggressive towards his teachers. Today I know that our children knew much more about the things that surrounded Dorit and me than we would have thought.

In the meantime something happened to Dorit end of the 2000's that I could not solve. She met a married young man on a party with friends with whom she fell in love. She revealed this after I confronted her due to a feeling of mine that something was wrong. Dorit herself then moved farther and farther onto her own path. Many tries of mine to mend things with Dorit did not end positively for me. Anyway, Dorit also tried again not to give up our marriage. My hope grew, as I was not ready yet to break things off. Too much was connected to it all and I was too connected to it all.

In 2001 I turned 50 and I decided to have a talk with Dorit after the big celebration. I decided to get the matter in a way where she could only end up with a clear 'yes' or 'no' from her side. A week after the party we looked for a neutral terrain for our conversation close to the edge of the woods, a place where we had been just the two of us many times out for more harmonious reasons. There I asked Dorit to permanently stop having affairs and especially to end things with her latest 'lover' Martin. Basically I knew all about everything all the time since Dorit always 'reported' in all honesty, when I asked her whether something was going on with anyone at the moment. That was our agreement. – I know, something like this is hard to understand, but I guess this was my way of trying to win back Dorit. – But this intention did not result in a happy end at all for me···

Getting back to our conversation: Dorit did not defer to my wishes to go back to be fully devoted to ourselves, to our marriage and family life. She asked me for 3 months of probation. In that time we wanted, next to other things, go on a 'love trip' to Bavaria and she wanted to enjoy some freedom with Martin (her lover). I agreed once more, hoping that I would win back Dorit for our life together.

Self-destructive – I am not a masochist, I am really not! What was happening to me then, I did not see it coming. Again many small and big cuts on my soul! Dorit went to see Martin whenever she wanted and whenever it was compatible with our family life. We spent a week holiday in Bavaria – but this could not be called a 'love trip' at all. As chance would have it Dorit revealed that her lover was in the very near at the same time to take a cure. At the same time we had our 'holiday', a collision of two airplanes occurred. That happened around 100 km away of our holiday spot and Dorit became really quiet when she heard of the disaster. I asked her about it and she told me then that that's the place where Martin was taking his cure. For me this disaster was a sign, a sign however that I didn't want to see at all. Unsatisfied with this trip and with deep anxiety I went towards the agreed last day of our 3 months' probation period.

Again we spoke openly.

Dorit told me she wanted to stay married – especially because Martin did not want to leave his wife. An incredible feeling of happiness rose inside of me. It was the beginning of September 2002 and I looked happily into the future – but then I felt a big discontent in Dorit. We talked about it and she said that she needed more time for all of this back and forth.

End of September everything seemed to be back to normal like in the good old times, Dorit turned me on and wanted sex with me. We hadn´t slept together since our 'vacation' – over 2 months ago. Horny as I was, suddenly she left me lying there. I do not imply she had bad intentions – she only said: 'I cannot sleep with you anymore!' – I felt down, very hurt and for the first time I verbally exploded··· I reached the end of the line. I ripped her clothes out of the closet, got her suitcases and shouted that she should leave. But only minutes later I apologized again and asked her to stay. She said that she could understand my outburst and slept in another room that night. I don´t remember if I could even sleep that night, but fell even more into the deep.

A few days later Dorit went to stay with friends in the neighboring town after all. She needed some space and I was constantly whining after her – there is no other way to describe this. After 3 days she came back, but informed me that she would take a psychosomatic cure in 3 weeks. Okay, I accepted this hoping that she would use the time to find the way back into our life. When she left she cried and told me that she would rather stay. At the beginning we had some nice phone calls and then all of a sudden she was unreachable for me – I could not get in touch with her. Again my soul was aching – no thought of depression from my side. Somehow I still had energy and made a decision. I finally reached Dorit after all and I told her that we had to make a final decision. With this intention I also connected new hope again, since I knew Dorit now for 30 years and I knew that she would rather leave the decision to me, so I hoped that she would respond to me and stay.

The agreed day, end of November 2002, arrived. Dorit was still taking her cure. The phone called in the evening. Dorit informed me that she would not be coming home afterwards, and that is what happened. – I felt somewhat of a relief back then but also a deep grief that everything didn't turn to the better···

Two weeks later when she came back, she went straight to her friends, who offered her a room. Incredible was that only 2 days after our 'phone call of decisions' I received a letter from a lawyer demanding alimony, and this letter was written before our agreed 'appointment' to make a decision···

Now the divorce battle begins

Since then the year was nearly over. Close to Christmas I decided that I did not want to stay alone at home over the holidays even when my daughter, who meanwhile lived on her own, said she would come to me over the holidays. My son had a girlfriend where he spent most of his time··· - I booked a flight to the Dominican Republic – to the Caribbean – summer feeling in the winter. For me that was really a new feeling – alone on 'vacation'. Maybe the distance would help, help to find distance.

Beforehand I can say that I was physically far away but could never find the distance in that time. I was thinking again and again everything, everything that had been and that could have been...

Many years of 'fight' for love and happiness and because you wanted to live together and because you didn't want to lose – all of that was behind me! What was in front of me? I also had good thoughts because these where promising new times – without this burden. 'Without this burden?' I wasn't able to think that far yet, what was laying in front of me then and how weakened my soul was···

The flair and everything around, what I experienced in the Dominican Republic was lovely. A great atmosphere and even Christmas feelings! It was decorated to look a little like Christmas there, too and they constantly played songs that would not let you forget Christmas. I also couldn't forget the reason why I was there. 5 days before my return (3rd of January 2003) I was sitting on the balcony in front of my room. It was a warm evening and as it is common in the Caribbean, already dark at 7 pm. Suddenly I had a panic attack. I didn't understand why I was there, where I was and I also wondered why··· I couldn't reach the answer and I couldn't understand it, that reality – I wanted to get away. The next day I asked at the reception for a number of a German travel agency. I called them and wanted to book a flight back home. – This kind of real panic is hard to describe. It was similar to the event back in the barn at the wedding, as I described in the beginning··· just a slightly different reason. The German travel agency told me that it was not possible – on such short notice··· -

I calmed down a little bit and came back to my senses. I told myself that I could hold on a few more days and when I would be back in Germany I would talk to Dorit right away and try to mend things with her.

When I was back home – alone as never before – a lot of mails stacked up! Along with it came a letter from the Internal Revenue Service. Dorit was acting fast to get the tax categories changed, which was complete bullshit, because this way we both gave away money to the state. People who know about those things also described this to me like this. I slowly realized what was awaiting me also because discussions I had with Dorit about how to handle a divorce on our own had been sterile and unregenerate. She gave it all away to lawyers and other people who in her opinion advised her better···

I was thinking about starting to make new connections in the meantime. Connections to other women! My thoughts went as far as to think about how my future woman should look like, and how her character ought to be. So I started to look for adverts in the newspaper and advertised myself as well. In February 2003 it came to a phone call and a meeting. But for me nothing further happened. I think I wasn' t really open for something like this back then. Looking back in the past, I would say that a man has to be taken by the hand after a separation like this. He should be kept away from those ambitions to dash into something new. The next months should prove that.

A new beginning – and it went on downwards

Beginning of March my daughter was visiting, she was also single at the time. We talked about that and I told her that I was already looking in newspapers for new affairs. My daughter then explained to me that there were quite good platforms on the Internet for that purpose and we registered an account on one of those sites for me. A platform 'only' to meet new people.

Very soon afterwards, I already had some nice legitimate contacts. End of March beginning of April it got more serious with a beautiful woman that was 20 years younger than me and who showed great interest in me. That flattered me a lot. We talked on the phone and this fresh connection got quickly deeper. I will call her Maren here – Maren was an independent web designer, divorced and mother of 2 girls who were 4 and 7 years old at the time. She lived about 150 km away from the town I lived in. – It moved fast for her and so she was standing in front of my door one evening. A very attractive woman and I had a hard time coping with this situation. Inside of me I felt inferiority complexes that had grown over the past 15 years. Maren took away many of these complexes almost immediately, at least for the following 2 days and nights, in which she stayed with me. I do not want to hide here that I also did have some problems with my manhood··· - Since end of September, after my ex had interrupted having sex with me I hadn't been with a woman and this experience was vividly inside of me··· for a long time.

Maren was good at handling this though because we also talked about it. Talking to each other can sometimes open many doors···

In the coming weeks we got to know each other even better and visited each other more often. I also noticed however that Maren was smoking and drinking a lot. She consumed up to 3 packs of cigarettes per day and many times up to an entire bottle of brandy per day. With all those feelings that had grown inside of me I started a conversation with her about this soon. She was undiscerning and knew how she could soothe me. Extreme time came towards me··· After about 2 months I broke things off and found myself a new and unproblematic friendship with a woman called Katja. Only a short time later － 4/5 weeks － Maren had caught me back. All was a back and forth from today＇s point of view, what I didn＇t realize back then. Meanwhile I moved out of my house and closer to Maren. My ex and I then strived to sell our house.

About Dorit － her lawyer started sending me more and more demands and letters where I was asked to prove this and that about my financial status. Those were all stabs in the back for me. My son demanded alimonies through a lawyer to support his life as well － even though my ex and I had arranged an agreement with him in that matter. In the meantime I hired a lawyer myself who was supposed to plead for my interests. With my son I had a discussion, which was very intense but in the end we were laying in each other＇s arms, crying.

Because our property was left behind, it started to go rack and no one wanted to buy it. I decided after only 2 months to move back into the house. Maren also moved out of her house because she could not keep up her financial status. It was now easier for me to meet her as she lived a little closer to me.

In this time － September/October 2003 I still felt disturbances inside of me － weakness about nearly everything and crying fits that came ＇out of the blue＇. Furthermore my blood pressure was extremely high. I consulted about all of this with my doctor, who recommended me to consult a psychiatrist. She gave me a list with addresses. I called all of them – approximately 15. First appointments were given only in about 3-4 months. Hopelessness grew inside of me and I was not able to follow up my profession any longer. In the middle of October it got so bad that I did my best to receive more help. My doctor finally achieved and made an appointment with a psychiatrist for me immediately. He distinguished the situation and the word 'depression' finally came up – deep depression. He recommended me to commit myself into a clinic so they could help me. After I asked him to help me in this matter, he personally called a clinic and organized everything for me. I got an appointment for only 3 days later in a 'private-nerve-facility' - a specialized clinic with psychiatric ward and psychotherapy. Everything was handled with my health insurance beforehand.

Maren supported me tremendously on this first step that I was planning and said that she raised her hat to me for it. She had never been able to do this and she knew that especially men do not easily own up to the ' " weaknesses" of having a depression. That was something special. I did not see it like that. I just wanted to get out of that darkness.

What had happened in the past couple of years!?

- After years of back and forth and over 25 years of marriage my wife had left me
- I suffered from 'dissociative disorder' for quite some time
- I went on a 'panic-vacation' during Christmas time at the Caribbean
- Meanwhile letters and demands of my ex-wife's lawyer arrived

- I searched for new relationships with women
- A new relationship formed with a woman who was 20 years younger and was not able to handle her own life well
- "Helper syndrome' grew inside of me
- I moved out of my house into a flat
- After 2 months in the flat I moved back into the house
- All was carried out with many physical and financial efforts
- I carried out my profession even though
- I also had great trouble with my son
- I broke up with Maren and started a new relationship
- Then I broke up with the new woman and went back to Maren
- Maren moved and that had to be done
- Etc. etc. etc···

···Then came the meltdown···

From today's point of view all that was not ME, who acted. I see myself as a marionette back then. A strange power had me in its clutch – it was leading me- chaotic! Why don't you recognize this yourself in a situation like this? And there weren't any friends or relatives who said: 'Hey, what are you doing? Come back to the ground! Search and find a better way!'

Now I was in the clinic and focused on the therapy, but I did not have the feeling that they were working for me. I felt like controlled remotely. During my time there I received a message from an unknown person. It was the wife of my ex-wife's lover. Where she got my mobile number from was a mystery to me. She wrote that she would not let her husband leave and many other things on this topic – many times she bombarded me with these messages and asked me many questions. Inside of me hope grew again and I thought that my marriage might be saved after all··· - After 4 weeks – too soon – I decided that I would discontinue my stay at the clinic. I thought that I had to go back into my life. I did not want to lose anything that was left there. My work – my new love, maybe my old love···

Maren had sent me a letter to the clinic. In that she confessed that she had severe psychological problems herself and that she tried to suicide once. She was raped when she was 18 years old on the street and she had never shared this with anyone. She also wrote that I was very important to her and that her children liked me a lot.

When I was back with her, she and her girls told me that they would like to live with me. I felt new strength and it touched me positively, especially since Christmas was approaching···

I felt, however, that my employer, for whom I had worked for nearly 15 years, kept distance with me. I had a new boss, a very unpleasant person. My previous boss knew about my problems and supported me. He gave me time and the chance to deal with many things on the side. Sincerity was very important for it. Unfortunately he was laid off, shortly before I went into the clinic. Now many things changed in the company, particularly since other hierarchies were also filled with new personnel. A so called 'generation change' occurred. They explicitly told me that my personal problems were not to be connected to my professional life – basically (quite) okay···

I spent a lot of time with Maren and her girls now. I took over Marens financial problems in the meantime. I earned well. A few weeks later, in the New Year 2004, Maren and I started to have a dream together. We wanted to purchase a hotel and enter the catering business to 'free' ourselves from everything. The seller provided an attractive financing offer. We visited the object and discussed all details. We had already received a purchase agreement. Because Maren had a bad credit score I had to be responsible for everything. My head was not clear enough back then. I saw not only the financial pressure, I also saw the problems Maren had with alcohol and her high cigarette consumption··· - That alone made up a sum of 700 Euros per month. I decided against that 'dream' of independence and told Maren that I could not provide the financial security, especially since the whole divorce business was still ahead of me.

Out of this situation Maren and I decided that she and her kids should move in with me. This way we were going to have more structure and that was what we did end of May 2004, so another move was to be managed··· Maren came with the girls into my house. My ex-wife accepted that because then the house would not be given to strangers···

The divorce was still going on. Visits from lawyers, letters here and there from my ex-wife's lawyer and the court. It was mainly about financial statements that I had to proof etc. I can remember EVERYTHING precisely but one thing additionally happen to me in that time – I grew a defense against all those statements and written proofs and against all of this bureaucracy. A kind of phobia arose – a phobia I still have today in a way.

Beginning of April 2004 it finally happened. After almost precisely 30 years my marriage was ended and yet I was confronted bureaucratically for another 2 years after that until finally my ex-wife's financial demands were 'fulfilled'.

In the meantime problems with my superior grew. In hindsight I would call what happened there mobbing, I was monitored extremely in everything I did and I also had to hand in uncommon reports and solve uncommon tasks. Then the company requested my presence and it was located 500 km away from my residence. Nobody told me why. As naïve as I was, I thought, that this was about an expansion and an improvement of my current range of duty. It was not like that. Sitting together with all superiors and the works council, I felt like standing against the wall with everybody pointing their guns at me··· Shortly, they were going to let me go. But that wasn't so easy··· Arriving back at home I received a lot of emotional help from Maren and I hired a labor unions lawyer. Finally, I gave up due to my weakness and agreed to a termination of employment – with a decent compensation and the contract continued for another 3 months with payments etc. and my ex wife also still had claims for all of it···

In this time I was on sick leave. I found myself around in this situation, hoping to find a new job soon, because I was known to be reliable and good at what I do···

In addition, another blow of fate occurred then. My daughter (I will call her Lara here) had had health problems for a while back then – additionally her self-employment did not work out as she was hoping and wishing for. Lara had a full medical examination and it turned out that she had MS (multiple sclerosis). Possibly she was still in the first stages of this terrible illness but her attacks led her into a low. She didn't know how it would go on. She was like paralyzed and required psychological help. I contacted her health insurance who placed her into a psychiatric clinic in the neighborhood. This facility, however, was more for people with permanent mental illnesses but she was in good hands. I could gain new strength to take further steps for her. After many efforts I received a spot for her in the

'private-nerve-clinic' where I had been end of 2003. That was a better place for her and my ex-wife also agreed with it···
Now it was July 2004.

Maren, her kids and I lived like a real family. Maren recognized her problems more and worked on reducing her vice. Between us it was like a real nice young love···

Meanwhile we had summer holidays – July 2004. We had had a nice week in Denmark and decided to buy a little dog. The girls had also found some friends whom they were seeing. The older one was on holidays at her aunt′s. Maren and her younger daughter and I had a nice breakfast on the terrace on Saturday. We discussed some things that had to be taken care of. After the breakfast I went to buy groceries. The younger daughter of Maren went to visit a friend in another close village. I returned around noon. Maren wasn′t there··· I thought that she had gone for a walk. My house was directly next to a forest. I went to a bench close to the forest, where we usually sat. But I did not find her. When I arrived back at the house I saw something white around 50 meters away in between the woods. Maren had a white sweatshirt. I called out and ran right over. Of course many thoughts went through my head···

··· Maren was lying next to a tree – as if she was sleeping. I tried to shake her to wake her up, I tried to ventilate her mouth to mouth··· I ran to the phone and called an ambulance··· Everything happened as if I was in trance!

Maren had departed from this life.

The doctor later told me that her central nerve system was paralyzed. For that you need specific pills··· which ones exactly, nobody could tell me···

After what had happened that day, Marens daughter was picked up by her relatives and my close friends already left, I was sitting on the bench on my terrace and recalled the happenings··· if I had had the same pills in that moment, I wouldn´t have been here any longer···

A night without sleep was ahead and my little dog, as if she could feel what happened, snuggled up to me in the bed···

The next day I drove the 160 km to Marens relatives. I immediately felt coldness and that I was not welcome there. So I drove back home, and was alone. I went to the spot where Maren had taken her life and smoked a cigarette with her – I had been a non-smoker until then. I just wanted to be close to her. That started out to be my ritual for the following days -3 times per day.

I slipped into the deep – deeper and deeper. I tried not to see anyone because every meeting with acquaintances or friends led to crying fits. Every step was like a lead weight, every action without strength – everything was so emotionless – everything without prospect. I went back to look for medical advice.

2 weeks after Maren's death, I went back into a psychiatric clinic – the same as in the end of 2003, the same where my daughter was now··· - A very special situation! My daughter and I in the same psychiatric clinic! But we were supposed to keep our contact to a minimum. Once a day we would meet, often in the community house. – The stay at that clinic was good for both of us. I felt that my daughter gained her strength back and for me it was the distraction··· It felt also good that I did not have to take care of anything – almost anything···

Maren wanted a cremation, as her close friends told me. The funeral was almost 4 weeks after her death. I got to know about the appointment more or less by coincidence. I wanted to go there and received a special permission for it from the clinic. Maren's ex-husband gave her urn to me so I could carry it to her grave. He and the girls where the only ones left with whom I still felt a connection. That day also passed and I returned to the clinic. I hoped for myself that after the funeral peace would set in··· it was not like that (yet)!

Time in the deep – emptiness – and the first steps back out...

My daughter was discharged of the nerve-clinic by the beginning of September. I decided also to leave the clinic at that time. That way we left both together. Lara and I planned to go on a vacation together. That should give us back some strength. Lara loved Italy and so we went there for a week at the beginning of October. We drove to many historical sites and enjoyed the time. We also talked about Lara's future. She decided to give up everything she had in Germany and to accept a job as some kind of geriatric nurse in England. She wanted to start doing that in 2005. – How it would go on for me was uncertain. When I was back a home alone I started to feel this weakness about doing anything more and more. I asked friends to support me with my chores around the house and garden. – I had no contact to my son…

We approached the end of the year again. I still had deep contact to Maren internally. I held on to the daily rituals, to smoke a cigarette three times per day in 'her spot'. I started reading books about this illness 'depression'. I read books about how to part from a deceased. Almost every night – when I felt like it – I would darken the living room, sit down and play music on the CD player that we both enjoyed. I only lit one candle on the living room table and looked at pictures of Maren. I talked to her, I ranted at her that she had left her children, that she didn't talk to me about her problems…

Maren was very excessive about a lot of things and then she could be very introverted and quiet. I wasn't familiar with any of those things beforehand. Now I knew that she was maniacal depressed!

In the meantime I started therapy with a psychiatrist and I took antidepressants. The pills did not have a good effect on me. I didn' t feel like myself anymore. Everything was dull, without emotions. The doctor said however that it was important to stick with it. Even a medical treatment takes its time, she said. I cooperated. Next we also applied for a 'cure'. Because the pension insurance and my health insurance were interested in getting me back into work, it was only right to go through a therapy in an appropriate clinic. I was only 53 years old after all.

Close to Christmas I had my appointment for admission into the 'clinic for psychosomatics and psychotherapy'. On their website they had written a nice wording: 'Life can only be understood backwards, but it must be lived forwards' – a quote by Sören Kierkegaard.

In this clinic I was supposed to stay for the following 6 weeks. At the end it was extended for another week and therefore I stayed 7 weeks. This clinic was surely not the number 1 on this field but the stay there helped me a lot – however, my personal willpower was also an important factor.

I wanted to get out of this LOW.

In the past 2-3 months I had gained 15 kg – among others a side effect of the antidepressants. I stopped taking the pills without my doctors 'permission'. I also started a diet where I ate half the amount of food. I did that very consequently. Additionally I used the fitness possibilities at home.

Maren would have had birthday on the 18th January. On that day, I said goodbye to her for good, in my room in all silence···

The 5 pillars of life

We speak of a positive structure in life if the so-called 5 pillars of life support the house of life.

The 5 pillars are:

Pillar: Job
The average working person spends half of their adult life working. Imagine, the job does not make you happy and is demotivating. That means, that you 'give away' half of your life. The other situation is the loss of your workplace···

Pillar: Finances
Finances are important, because they bring freedom. Dependency constrains···

Pillar: Health
Health is something that you only appreciate after it's gone···

Pillar: Relationships
A sorrow shared is a sorrow halved, and not only that··· To have a partnership in good and bad times is very important and helps immensely···

Pillar: What you are
This is your own personality and your self-esteem···

The collapse of only one of these pillars makes the house of life unstable··· - you could say, that my house of life could not be supported by any of those pillars any longer···

Now it was time for: Reconstruction!

Yes, I do!

At the time Peter Maffay (a German singer) published a song, which was called: 'Yes, I do!' That song helped me to look for ways to get back on top. – Sometimes you only need a sign and you have to recognize this sign to be able to follow the way···

As if I got a broad hint from 'above', I started having a nice pleasant contact to a fellow patient. Until then, I did not have interest in the opposite gender and was only busy with myself···

It was only the contact and the many nice conversations that we had, which made me feel 'alive'. I saw that other people also had extreme problems. Conversations help. To share gets rid of a lot.

The depression inside of me was still there. There were many times, especially in the morning, when emptiness filled me. I tried to fill the emptiness by calling friends or family, just to talk. From time to time I also suffered from 'dissociative disorders'. Additionally, from 2005, I had 'ophthalmic migraine' – the so-called 'eye-migraine', which I couldn't make out back then. For about half an hour something like a little crystal is floating in front of your eye, which is growing bigger until it disappears. After that I was always extremely sensitive to light and noises for about 1-2 days. I did not know what it was and only 2 years later, in a conversation with my psychiatrist, it was explained to me. Those migraine attacks have stayed with me until today, the 'dissociative disorder' and the 'perspiration attacks' have been disappearing more and more, but only since 2009 I can say that they are completely gone.

Now back to the beginning of 2005.

After my stay in the clinic I felt stronger, but not strong enough. It was too much inside of me and not all of it was gone. But I wanted change. So I decided after written consultation with my ex-wife, who in the meantime lived with her 'lover', that the house needed to be sold. I wanted to start over in the big city of the surrounding area. Close to that city lived Bea with her family, the nice fellow patient from the cure. We kept in touch – but later more.

I found a buyer for the house soon. He received it in May 2005 for a price way under value. – Before, I organized a so-called garage sale and sold nearly everything, especially since I found only a small attic apartment for my future life, close to the city and close to my family, for rent.

I felt very comfortable in my 'new life' there. I made a living with what I got from my health insurance. I made a plan about how it had to go on. I wrote about 30 applications for companies that were acceptable for me. Without success! Time passed by. Because so many people had told me that I was a good listener over the past few months I was thinking about becoming a therapist myself. I checked for information about my possibilities and found a career as 'conversational therapist'. With the help of the employment office, which supported me with a special program, I got a degree by correspondence course in that field. For about 18 months it was supposed to last. I felt good about these requirements. But I searched for some side jobs anyway, worked at a wine merchant and went from door to door to attract new customers and for a frozen-food delivery service.

In addition, my circle of friends grew around family and friends of Bea – that was good, and it felt good. I had new friends and something like a family. I also got along well with my landlord.

People grow older and I took care of their gardens.

Therefore, all in all I was relatively busy then.

On a bumpy way...

Fall 2006 arrived and it was time. I got my degree. I was now offering my expertise as conversational therapist through an advertisement paper and flyers. I could easily prepare one of the rooms in my flat for this. Soon clients started to come. I enjoyed this line of work – but soon I noticed that I was financially not prepared to pay my living with this for long term and after only 3 months I stopped this venture "conversational therapy".

I felt that I slipped back down a little. I did not see financial stability for my future. I always saw welfare (Hartz 4= a social help in Germany) in front of me and my situation blocked me from making new interpersonal contacts – a woman on my side.

I went back to see my psychiatrist. The first months of 2007 passed by! Not a nice time until I received a suggestion by my psychiatrist, to contact my pension insurance and ask about whether early retirement – the so called 'reduced earning capacity pension' – was an option for me. I did that and was told what kind of requirements you have to fulfill in order to receive it. I felt overwhelmed by the amount of forms. Since the days of my divorce I was blocked against these bureaucratic activities··· forms, applications etc. My psychiatrist helped me and informed me that there was a 'social union' to help with these tasks. And then everything went on relatively fast. First we figured out that I had to go back to a clinic again for another stay to support my proposition. So I went to a very good clinic for another 5 weeks in June/July 2007 close to the Weser river. After that, in July 2007, I turned in the papers, with the help of the social union, to the pension insurance. Only 4 weeks later I received the positive answer, that from September 2007 I was going to receive 'reduced earning capacity pension'.

Like a fat big stone a burden fell off of me. Even if I do not receive a huge amount of pension, it was enough to live from it and pay rent.

This situation solved a lot for me. I had a basis with which I could go on and I still worked a little on the side for my landlord, I cleaned the hallways and had 100 Euros more at the end of the month.

Now I tried slowly to get in touch with the other sex again. With the help of the Internet this is easily possible and there are reliable platforms for it. On the other hand I am not a person who is very fast in these things. My not so far away past had taught me that at least. It took some time with some nice chats and phone calls until a meeting for coffee came to be. In the following months I had a few more dates but I felt blocked to do more – especially as I had a big fear of failing, which had built up over the past years…

In the first months of the year 2008 I thought a lot about how I could earn some more money on the side because I didn't feel I was using my entire capacity. My thoughts lead to me doing what I was good at doing before and what wouldn't overwhelm me, the word was 'gardening'. I knew gardening and it was fun for me.

In the meantime the contact to my son got better. We met every now and then since he lived close by. My daughter now jobbed for an Internet firm in Ireland after she had worked in England for a year.

In March 2008 I advertised in a regional paper and offered my help for gardening. Very soon I had 10 locations, mostly for older people, for whom I partially or completely did their gardens. In some cases my son even helped out. I had a job now that physically challenged me – that was good and additionally I made contact to people and we had nice conversations. Also this work helped my financial situation so that I was able to save up. Because my saving was used up over the past years – lawyer fees, a car had to be bought (before I had a company car) and additionally many costs for moving⋯

It seemed as if my world was (almost) all right again. I had a good relationship to my children, I liked my new neighborhood, I had nice friends and contact to many people and on top of that a financial stability. The 5 pillars, which secure your life, were (almost) completely back. 'Almost' – yes, 'almost' – because the emotional part was missing: A life partner!

I made a few more or less little 'tries'. Many times I felt in the background that those women also had 'past issues' which would not allow an uncomplicated relationship. I always ended these relationships quite fast. I, myself, did not feel fully free of the life I had for the past years – I was not ready yet! You do not shake off something like this so fast: 30 years of marriage, which dragged me down to the end and then a much too soon relationship with a younger woman, who had her own big problems and ended her own life – the loss of my workplace and therefore the loss of financial stability, my own weakness caused by depression and loss of property⋯

⋯ You don't move on from something like this easily, apart from this, I know today, that your past always stays with you – but the strength that you need for a fresh start sometimes comes unexpected⋯

The beginning of the new presence - or: 'Back to the roots!'

As the saying goes: 'Life can only be understood backwards; but it must be lived forwards.'

Because of the new ways and possibilities I felt better and better bit by bit:

I had a better and more secured financial basis in my life – therefore a future I could approach reassured.
My personal environment was much nicer due to my new friends and acquaintances
Physically and mentally I felt improvements

I read, in the beginning of May 2009, a message on Facebook sent by a woman (Tiana) who had the same surname as me and contacted me because of her family-chronicle research. She basically lived on the other side of the world, in South America and had German roots because of her great-grandfather. Her request was legitimate, I saw that right away. I have a family-chronicle that dates back to the 1680's. We could not, however, make out any similarities on our chronicles while we were chatting. Our name is quite rare and the place of residence of her and mine great-grandfathers was the same, but we were not related.

But Tiana and I had more and more nice chats and our interest in each other grew. Tiana was not attached emotionally and neither was I. To cut a long story short: I visited Tiana in the far country, where she showed me a lot about it and a lot about herself. Love grew fast for us and by the end of 2009; I cut all my ties in Germany and emigrated to her. And in those days of change old strengths woke inside of me. Everything that was connected to this move and all local tasks I had left to do, I handled with ease, and fast.

In the far away country I experienced a true fresh start, in all aspects. Tiana, who was in her early 40's back then, and I were soon expecting a baby. In spring 2011 our little son was born. We decided quickly that our son should grow up in Germany and left the country end of March 2012, for good. Now we live together with our son happily in a beautiful home close to our original roots – 'back to the roots' ···

I do not want to leave out that I did experience weaknesses in the first 2-3 years with Tiana – surely no depression, but my fear of failing and fear of loss discomforted me. It simply took time and security that lead me to find back to my old self···

Summary

- Tried to keep love and marriage for more than 10 years, tolerated sexual excursions of wife
- First consequences: restlessness, perspiration attacks, first anxiety attack, dissociative disorders
- End of marriage
- Consequences: Depression
- Beginning of a new and complicated relationship
- Consequences: high blood pressure and continuity of existing health issues, drop in performance professionally
- Loss of workplace, unemployment, divorce, suicide of girlfriend
- Consequences: deep depressions, continuity of existing health issues, additionally migraine attacks, fear of loss, fear of failing
- Therapy with psychiatrists and curative treatments in clinics
- Consequences: slow recovery of mental strength.
- Rethinking own future, plan of recovery for a social and financial security, claim of early retirement, new life companion.
- Present condition – negative: no depression, minimal fears of failing, migraine attacks are left and strong issues with solving bureaucratic activities – positive: recovery of mental and physical strength, happiness in life and satisfaction.

Concluding sentences

What could my conclusion be from the experienced, from more than 20 years of my past?

Surely we are all very different. Many of our characteristics are formed in our first years in life. From my standpoint I can say that you should not get involved in games in your marriage or other areas of your life that would cross the line of 'normal'. Lines that you cross cost strength and cause loss of energy. If you lack of security, you create a basis for illnesses. The body will look for weak spots. Many illnesses are caused by psychosomatic problems. If you are at a point where many things are in pieces – for example a marriage – do not jump into something new right away. Take your time; time and patience, to process the things that have lead you to where you are now. Take your time, always, to recognize something. Knowledge gives security, knowledge shows you ways, and through knowledge you recognize more··· and accept help for it – help of qualified professionals.

Herbert W. Rode

Table of Contents